WATER WITCHING

# Water Witching

*poems by*

**Kathleene West**

*Copper Canyon Press*
*Port Townsend : 1984*

Grateful acknowledgment is made to the following periodicals and anthologies in which many of these poems first appeared:

Backbone; Intro, Jawbone Press Broadside Series; Jeopardy; Niagra; The Pacific; Poetry Northwest; Point Riders Press Anthology of Great Plains Poetry; Port Townsend Leader; Puget Sound Quarterly; Rapunzel, Rapunzel; Sandhills; Seattle Review; Slackwater Review; Spoor; The Three Seasons; Willow Springs; Woman Poet; and Yakima.

Several of these poems also appeared in No Warning (Jawbone Press).

Publication of this book is made possible in part by a grant from the National Endowment for the Arts, a federal agency. Copper Canyon Press is in residence at Centrum.

ISBN 0-914742-82-5
Library of Congress Catalog Card Number : 84-71254

The type is Perpetua, set by Irish Setter.

Copper Canyon Press
P.O. Box 271
Port Townsend, WA 98368

FOR MY SISTER
*Barbara Imig*

# CONTENTS

## A Woman Defines

## Farmer's Child

## Water Witch

# A Woman Defines

## Pining Away as an Erotic Activity

I waste, like paper, in your absence,
insistent ribs and blades
straining toward the surface.
You could label me like a skeleton
on bones pale and lingering
as a street light. My fingers click
into a thin fist.

Nothing on hand, but a jar
of relish, to whet and unsatisfy
my hungering tongue. Weak and empty,
I watch visions like late movies,
turning to the restricted channels.
How perfectly I can tune you.

Faded to the color of smoke,
all my hair uncurls, long and straight
as grief. My body is hollow.
I hear echoes inside,
repeat, imitate, the last obsession,
a former touch.

## A Woman Defines

*"Want to see something funny? Tell a woman to put*
*her hands behind her and describe a brick."*
—Overheard at the construction company

I

A molded block of clay,
baked by the sun or in a kiln
until hard
and used
for building and paving.

She stands before him, each arm forming
a triangle. Once she listened to advice,
tried to live rectangular, but strains less
with hands that grow inward,
away from pavement and rough walls.

II

These blocks collectively.

She frames herself in the doorway,
a crooked picture. If he tries
to straighten her, they will merge.

III

*Informal.* A splendid fellow.

They discuss masonry and the merits of living
with bricks. An expert in edging,
he shows her how to place a border.
Later, she will steal the stones that trim
his garden and build a fireplace.

IV

In the expression,
"Make bricks without straw":
To try to do something
while lacking a needed component.

When the room grows colder, he presses
mud against the window, and she spreads dry grass
on the floor. As the mud dries, his skin cracks,
and dust spills down on her hands.

V

To close or wall with brick.
Usually used with *up*
or *in*.

During the growing season, she apprenticed herself
to a bricklayer and learned the difference
between up and in. As she builds the turret
around him, he is entranced by her skillful hands.
He does not notice her face, ruddy
and angular, like a brick.

A New Decade: Watching the Digital Clock
Advance Toward Midnight


She displays him like a dependable bauble,
the ornament that's hung
high on the tree
or the necklace that's never undone.


*sing a song of love dear*
*another night struck by*


Pleased to forsake all former resolve,
she preens by his side,
slips long fingers over his shoulder.
He neither accepts nor denies.


*sheet and dream and memory*
*caught in your cry*


For he takes up her hand
in disinterested caress
and she feels their skin warm
with the necessary presence
                            of each other.


*when the bed is ruined*
*the scraps begin to sing*


Poised in this room
like the fragile souvenirs on the mantelpiece,
too delicate to adjust or move,
they wait for midnight to kiss.


*wasn't that a pretty kiss*
*to think of now and then?*

## Celebrating Disaster

*The Sinking of Hood Canal Bridge,*
*February 13, 1979*

We remember destruction
from our uncollective pasts.
I say water. Too much rain
for a narrow creek and a herd of cattle
caught on the wrong side.
Dad and I walked the washed-out corn rows
to count the bloated bodies. Only 13.
But the biggest mass of death I'd seen.
Easily topped by the Columbus Day Storm,
*What if Mount Baker erupted?* and
*Aren't we due for an earthquake—a big one?*

*What a small disaster,*
the road spongy with branches,
Christmas wreaths undone,
and chunks of insulation flung to the edge
like stunned chickens.
We try to feel stranded, bring out the best,
circled around a table, flinging dice.
*The object is to conquer the world,*
the world, the other side of that submerged bridge.
With each turn, palms warm, lines converge or fork,
depending on the reader.
No one thinks to mention fire.

Weeks later, a friend calls
to remind us.
*What did you lose?*
*Everything.*
Burnt with his cabin, books, manuscripts,

most of his past. And some of ours.
*God's a harsh editor.*
That's meant to be cheerful.
Nothing to give up
but delete *here*
                and *here*.

What's difficult is finding what remains.
Leave on the bedside light
and guess the dark patches—shadows
or bruises. Someone will see
which guess is right.

*Poem on Losing One's Hair*

*—after Han Yü*

Even when Mother tapped my head
and it *thunked* like a ripe melon,
I wouldn't believe her.
When a roomful of people
stood over me, poking
with cold fingers, I believed
but refused to look.

In this loft, I held up a glass,
backed toward the mirror.
Tree lit a match.
"Don't scream," she said.

I never thought
age would attack this way.
Gray hair—wrinkles.
Some bizarre behavior.
I hoped for a rare disease
or a common one.
"You've plenty of hair," the doctor said.
"Just comb some over."
I tried not combing
to preserve what remained.
Some said goat's milk,
but I didn't know whether to swallow
or pour it over my head.

I'm looking hard for advantages.
If I lose all,
I see obvious savings in shampoo
and vanity.
But my hair divides
over a single spot

where I can balance a bottle cap
or the bottle.
It is larger.

I think of the beauty of patchwork
and embroidery over worn threads,
the thousands of tasks
for old cloth
and the stories to weave
over each mark and break
on my skin.

Here is a place, untouched,
unsung, where something shivering
waits for cover.

*Scars*

In high school, Marianne Lewis scratched
G R on her wrist
with a common pin,
kept on Gary Rubin's class ring
with a rubber band wrapped to cut
deep into her flesh.

> *When we break up,*
> *I'll still have the scar.*

You wonder
and I'm embarrassed to say
this scar's from falling up the steps.
I sent the Cahill kids in for Kleenex, a Band-Aid
then a towel
while I searched for a missing piece of skin
to patch the slice on my thigh
but the youngest tattled
and Mother poured peroxide on the gash
and the neighbor lady insisted
"Shouldn't that have stitches?"
I hollered "No!"
and the blood bubbled up with the foam
and Mother said no
she let me have the scar.

Three things I ask about: scars,
old loves and land,
whatever marks or heals
a surface.
How steep shall we make the hill?
How undamaged the site?
I tell you I bruise easily
but you find and kiss each dark circle

and safe as a leaf
I drop down the slope of your arms
pleased
momentarily healed
by this common miracle of our skin.

## Some Thoughts on May/December Romances
## And Other Frustrations

But Paul Newman is old enough to be my father too!
Damn the coincidence that gives
your oldest daughter my name!
It's like a second adolescence—
this clumsy stage
with the men my age still married
to their second wives
and those younger, still afraid.
The mirror assures me I am not
ridiculous and reminds me that once
at Baskin-Robbins a man said
I was beautiful.
But my face tightens like drying Clearasil
and my stomach knots to Friday nights in the gym,
pleated skirt and orlon sweater and Larry Pearson
dancing with Joanie Flaherty.
How dare you, my silvery darling,
cast me gawky and awkward?
I dance on a charcoal-wet sidewalk
with a sky to match.
In this country, my birthday is gray.
The seasons are reversible.

*Better an Old Man's Darling*
*Than a Young Man's Fool*


You watch his face, the lines that curve and swell
like sand ripples in the Baja desert. There,
the heat surrounds; it presses like the stare
of a solicitor and you think of the merry-go-round
at the Platte County Fair, riding the chestnut horse,
your legs stuck out stiff as a cornstalk, and watching
your father appear and appear as you spin.
Nothing blinks here. No lids or lashes, no power
to turn a complete circle. Watch his face.
You are a place of early fruit and fresh water
where the mesquite pushes its bloom
and the brittlebush chains daisies around you.
The branches dip and lurch, the wind
whirling the flowers like shrunken tumbleweeds.
Your body curls to follow. Crusted with sand,
it ripples, a half circle on the desert floor.

*Poem for Lonely Grammarians:*
*Copulative Verb Followed by Infinitive*

How clean it is
to be alone.

## A Few Comments on the Ventriloquist's Performance

How precisely you tongued his words,
lined your lips in a grin,
refusing to cheat, even in the dark,
mouthing the difference between you.

Listen to the versatile sounds stretch
and push each other,
a bird choking notes
out of its throat,
wind yearning at the door,
a bark from a dog who forgot
to challenge the moon.
Does it matter this dog twitched
all night in sleep,
denied its posture
on a moon-washed hill?
And you felt a heart
pumping too fast
beneath your fingers.
You felt. You felt.

Jar your teeth from the edge of the cup,
crack out a word or two
for practice, but when your skin
shudders you into silence,
listen again—
from beyond the skinny daylight trees
a demand thrown back
twisting in your mouth.

*The Poet Considers Destroying His Mailbox*


Thursday, and the mailbox gapes,
olive-drab, unexpectedly empty.
The afternoon's awry.
The toothbrush molts, coffee freezes
in the cup and veins on your wrist
push sullenly at the surface.
Your friends fling the telephone
out the window and slide out of your house
on the cord. Your lover walks up the stairs
and vanishes when she touches her hand
to the knob. Stamps won't stick. The avocado rolls
on the ledge, stays hard and green.
Did you really think the woman in the bar
would remember your number?
What did you expect? To hold love and work
like a blueprint in your hand?

## Marriage Contract: Allegory in the Kitchen

Straight and perfect, the plates congratulate
each other on their stacks.
Knives and forks segregate
in proper rows. The counter reminds the crumbs
of their obligation to summersault to the floor.
The floor urges the broom across its tile.
And the broom promises
a safe and pleasant landing out-of-doors.

But the sponge sighs; it feels used
and complains to the damp air
of drudgery, the degradation
of daily slime. Only the running water
can sympathize; it caresses the sponge
and sings of warm, dark seas
and tight colonies linked together
far from fluorescence and chrome,
bathed and safe on the irresponsible sand.

## Breakfast, Lighthouse Cafe

She eats circles of French toast
knifing each
into a round, blank hole.

Four corners of crust soak
on her plate, sodden brown angles
that point everywhere, except at her.

In his mouth, the eggs expand
like yeast, difficult to swallow
as a demand for love.

They speak in sharp, crisp words:
bacon, utensil, trout—
one trout, tricked from a black lake.

Her tough fork jabs
a last bite of syrupy bread.
Think of other empty circles—

thumb and forefinger
stalled clocks
the hoop dangling from a delicate ear.

## Current Event

*"Electric Women to Meet."*
—Seattle *Times*

Static, shock, a surge of power—
Electric women converge on the town.
A battery of women coil like wire.
Static, shock, a surge of power.

Circuits open, smooth as flour,
Ever-ready, they'll never run down.
Static, shock, a surge of power—
Electric women converge on the town.

## Woman Combing

*"It must
Be the finding of a satisfaction, and may
Be of a man skating, a woman dancing, a woman
Combing. The poem of the act of the mind."*
— Wallace Stevens

I should braid, tie back, bind this hair away
from you, but drawing half over each breast
I let the strands merge and fall like the manes
in a Clairol commercial. You muddle
and snarl my hair, with hands that mean
to fit things in place. And you say
I try too hard to be Rapunzel.

The first day to imagine spring,
I bent my head to the wind—comb, jerk
and pull through the mats on the back of my neck.
A handful ripped from the scalp,
and now my lines are again certain,
unwavering from crown to waist.
The mass of knots and snarl released
to the air, it bumps on shingles,
snared by the gutter. The sparrows fly by;
it is too confused for their nest.

Two days of bobbing on the rainspout,
and the tangle pulls free. I see it in the wind,
but the breeze dies, and my discarded hair falls
to the street. Bumping like a tumbleweed, it clings
to the wheel of a bicycle. I think
I see it catch and whirl on a spoke.

*For Cleopatra, Whose Name Should Not Be in a Poem*
*Because of the Associations*


But it's not your fault Mother ran off with the American,
and what had you to do with being the first born?
An old method: name the baby for the disowning grandmother,
and she'll forgive. With her Greek legacy and a Southern accent,
you practice forgiving alone.

How many times have you listened to: "It's not really your name!"
or explained, "No, it's not Cleo."
Taking and discarding names from father, stepfather
and two husbands, you still haven't found a surname
to match. Grandmother knew. Arranging love for you,
she beckoned the young man from Athens.
Was it your American half rebelling,
affirming the freedom of your winter skin?
Or the fear of becoming Greek too soon?

In Montana, I dedicated a poem to you,
and ten poets sitting around a table shook their heads, No!
The name suggests too much.
Consider Shaw, Shakespeare, the legends.
If you must dedicate, use the initial,
or omit the name completely.

My dear "C",
my sister,
I strike surnames and each month send a letter east
to Cleopatra.
The mirrors need cleaning, you write.
Your hands fly like frightened chickens, scratching
at your hair, to mask your face.

Remember the night you woke, hearing Greek music.
and crept downstairs to watch Grandfather
pacing folk dances on the rug. Drawing you
from the shadows, he pulled you closer

and guided you in his steps.
Tonight, after reading this,
stand alone in your house
and recall those steps. I will stand by you,
my hand on your shoulder, and we will dance.

## April Fool, Aphrodite

Fool me. Deceive me.
Stand on the right and tap my left shoulder.
Hang up when I answer the telephone.
Disappear from the opened door.
Touch my face while I sleep, hover over me—
what a ludicrous specter you are, like the puppet ghosts
we fashioned as children, wrapping a handkerchief
around a sucker.
You haunt me with the wrong season.
You should heap my bedroom with maimed ladybugs
and cabbage moths limping on my wrist, send
stillborn lambs and kittens in a parade
across my pillow.
I can't accept these jokes, can't believe
the rusty leaf dizzy in the descent,
the cracked hand, the blood line on the map
all beckon for me.

# Farmer's Child

## Pastoral

Spavined mule, scouring calves
Breech-birth, bloat, erysipelas
Rats in the corn crib, sheep in the corn
Little Boy Blue, come blow your horn.

Rusted wheat, potato bugs
Hoppers, corn borers, nematodes
Hornets in the outhouse, gophers in the lane
Little Boy Blue, come wish for rain.

Corn-cob fuel, stinkweed milk
Nettles, cockleburrs, creeping Charlie
Floods in the pasture, cows on the run
Little Boy Blue, come pray for sun.

Boiled tongue, fried-up heart
Wash tub, corn shucks, bread & lard
Mice in the attic, ringworm on the arm
Little Boy Blue just sold the farm.

*Farmer's Child*


That winter a farmer walked in pain
from a twisted back and the land he worked—a land
that glistened like a Christmas card, the barn
decorated with snow, flanked by steam-breathing cows,
impatient, bellowing to leave the cold
to barter grain for milk.

Lined like children, the cats yowled for milk.
A careful kick and they caterwauled in pain,
shaking their paws back to the cold,
reminded again: his rules, his land.
He called out to the cows,
and watched them sway like elephants into the barn.

A shadow loomed in each stall in the barn,
and the damp smell of hide and the hint of milk
pressed the air. He chained the cows,
this morning, gently, and the chain rubbed no pain.
Like others crouched in barns in this rough land,
he flexed his fingers in the morning cold.

No gloves for this task. His hands shook as the cold
and wheezing wind hooked through the barn—
one more message from his land.
Hunched like a cat over milk,
he paused as if to give the pain
a chance to grip before he bent to the cow's

bulging side. Between two solid cows,
he breathed a barrier against the cold,
imagined a barrier between pain
and his meager shadow cast to the barn
with a shadow bucket of grayish milk.
He thought of warmth in a windless land.

I've trailed behind you, my father, on this land
you own, or that owns you, herded the cows
down the pasture lane and balanced to milk
beside you. I know the fear that crawls with the cold
and the despair of a sagging, unshingled barn.
It's more than your back that brought you pain.

The land waits in a scene that is always cold.
Cows stamp fitfully in the barn.
The milk flows, smooth and steady as this pain.

## The Poet Becomes a Homesteader

I wanted the country
first. I wanted it empty.
Pushing beyond the last plowed field
to the unsettled sod,
I tried to fill it with my dreams.

No, never lonely.
But after years of bone and dust,
I found I was not enough.

## After Matchbox Funerals, Stock Trucks & Elegies in the Pasture

Not many old animals on a farm. Sometimes
the watchdog's smart enough
not to chase machinery
or a prize cow tops the milk bucket
one more season. An occasional wily cat.
These earned their names
and I call them out:

Colonel Doberman
Old Roan
Gray Whiskers

Each spring a farm bleats and squeals—impatient
with new animals.
I name as many as I can mark.
This year the orphaned pig is Joseph.
Rose Red, the delicate Guernsey heifer.
And Chicken Little, the timid Leghorn
that won't rush to the feeder.
I can't stop the baby chicks
from piling up in the corner
and smothering the one I meant to protect.
Between midnight and dawn,
a sow devours the runt.
The calf falls down on its knees.

Some lived long enough to recognize me,
ran on shaky legs
when I brandished the Nehi bottle of milk.
Converted to lamb chops and sausage,
they prospered the table.
Looking the other way,
I passed the platters of what used to be
Bobtail or Slurpy
and vowed I'd name nothing more
and care only for what grew in gardens.

## Cattle Call

Around a pasture,
you won't see new, tight fence.
A creosote post leans out of its hole,
sags the barbwire down
and the wire mesh stretches
as the cows kneel to ease their heads under, sideways,
ears scraping the ground
as if they listen to what goes on below.
Saliva streams out like spider silk
as the gray tongue strains to enwrap
the furthermost mouthful of firegrass.

Dad watches in disgust:

> Same goddamned *weeds* on both sides
> but they've still got to go & try.
> Come on kid, let's tighten her up
> so they don't get out this time
> but like I always say
> if you raise cows
> you're gonna chase 'em.

If cows weren't so stupid, you'd know
they orchestrated the best moment
to escape boundaries.
Sunday morning, in bed till it's light,
thinking of pancakes
and an hour in church, just to sit,
and someone up for water at the kitchen sink
hollers, "The cows are out!"

Or after hauling bales,
a cool evening bath to wash off the sticky itch,
leaning back in a kitchen chair
hungry at last

for fried meat and potatoes
and a huge white form sways
delicately by.
Forks clatter down, chairs drop—

    Move the skillet!
    Where's my shoes!
    Who in the hell left the cowlot gate open?

Everyone's cows got out.
I asked Dad why we didn't brand.
Knee-deep in Skeedee mud we were,
stretching (again) the wire across the bank.
Second flood that year.

    Hand me a staple, kid.
    Branding won't keep a cow from getting out.
    And it's not the worry over someone stealing one that does.
    I never let 'em get too far.
    Or even mixing with another herd
    —I sureashell know *my* cows—
    as the trouble when someone else's cow gets *in*.

    Hokansons, now, used to turn a couple of calves
    in our pasture, and they'd bounce up the lane
    just as pretty, eating our grass
    and our hay in the cowlot,
    ornery little cusses I remember,
    weren't dehorned, fighting with the heifers.
    Not worth it to rile neighbors
    but Mom painted something
    on those calves with green paint.
    Didn't tell me till later
    and never did say what she painted,
    figured I'd get mad.
    That Irma, she's a corker.
    Damnedest woman I ever saw.
    Well, Hokansons pulled 'em out fast.
    I tell you, kid, branding's not

what keeps a cow,
not in little operations like ours.

No matter if they run through the mud of the plowed field
or the gravel road to town,
circle wide around them, get ahead
and wait, arms outstretched,
maybe holding a stick
to make your arms longer.
Say you weigh 100 lbs.
say the cow weighs 1000
and is running.
You shout something in cow-turning language
like *Hike!*
or *Get Back!*
You imagine looking up at four hooves
printing their route over your body.
You imagine Dad's anger if you let the cow thunder by.
Your life depends
on turning this cow.

I don't know what people pray for.
Dad, I suppose, prays for—or to—sun and rain
just enough at the right time.
Mom prays the kids won't do anything bad enough
to get talked about in town.

And I pray when I'm frightened,
bartering promises to be a better person
for my long life and safety.
And chasing cows,
I prayed and promised most.

## Song for Two Voices

*Old woman, old woman, will you do my mending?*
*Speak a little louder sir, I'm very hard of hearing.*

When the noise beyond the haystack softened
to munch and snuffle, and the coyotes moaned,
pretending they cased the farm,
Grandma Linnerson moved the rocker into a circle of light
and bent over her fancywork.
They say she wasn't a proper wife,
never cooked a breakfast,
never rose to chip ice in the basin, always kept
a part of herself secret.

*Old woman, old woman, will you live to comfort me?*
*Speak a little louder sir, I cannot see your lips move.*

Shrinking a little each year, Granny Addie tried
to disappear. Like cottonwood leaves in November,
she withered, she crackled. Grandpa Roy swept the floor
and married again, a fine wedding this time
with a diamond and the Greyhound to Omaha.
In the picture, he stands behind the bride,
touching her sleeve.
The veins divide her hand like a leaf.

*Old woman, old woman, will you do the cooking?*
*Speak a little louder sir, your teeth are on the table.*

Lined in K & F, I relinquish my place to a woman
with tuna and Sweetheart soap. She squints
at my forehead, says she knew a Capricorn
would be kind. Her daughter's unhappy,
it's that Gemini husband and the child

conceived in the wrong month,
but those who need to believe never will.

> *Old woman, old woman, will you come and walk with me?*
> *Speak a little louder sir, your wheezing keeps me distant.*

When the light blinks green, my mother reaches for my arm.
I remember hating to hold her hand in public,
the agony of her presence. Now she trusts
I won't hurt myself, but why, as we leave the curb,
do I begin to cry?

> *Old woman, old woman, what's the use? the bother?*
> *Speak a little softer sir, you know I've always heard you.*

## Sister in a Restored Town

*for Darlene*

I cross a continent to find you, my sister,
in a house that castles you above Williamsburg,
but it's the town that belongs in a fairy tale.
Dead for a hundred years, the village breathes now,
awakened by a Rockefeller. After fire, rot
and that moneyed kiss, the town grew back,
but there's more here to unearth
than old foundations.

It's moving that makes things die, my sister.
If you read the guide book,
you envisioned the ruin
when the people fled inland. This town feeds
on history, the rebuilt walls steeped
with the must and mold of the past.

Do you remember the pact we made—never to marry?
And how I broke it when I turned eight,
thinking it a betrayal to my dollhouse family?
When you brought him home,
I felt so guilty, as if, young and conforming,
I'd failed you.

Again, failure. If I turn myself to wax,
I'm Queen Anne or Martha Jefferson,
smoother going back to a revolution
than a childhood.
With the pain of war forgotten,
your town stirred from rubble to an excavator's dream.

All's restored, my sister.
They have furnished the house
and the authorities of the heart
vouch for the authenticity of love.

*For a Long Winter*


I've always changed the fruit to store it,
boiling strawberries into furious jam,
flinging yeast over cling peaches
to bubble into wine, testing
the way of preservation.

Fruit moves too fast
from ripe to rotten. Dried pliable
in sun and air, it shrinks
leathery and wrinkled
but true as any Red Delicious on the branch.

Cupboards read like a museum:
Marmalade. Chutney.
North Orchard Pears.
The colors jell
in a year's worth of hoarded glass,
soft, deep colors of a healing wound.

Stir, turn,
holding what we love. Now
the compote melds its winter flavors.
Something settles on a shelf.

## Penmanship

*"What we have learned is not what we were told."*
—Weldon Kees

Miss Alice Ramakers arranged my fingertips,
pointed them straight down the barrel
of the fat, black pencil
and threatened to keep me after school for a week,
one week, to teach me how to write.
I cried, told her a milk cow stepped on my good hand,
forced my fingers into a death grip.
The story held water,
and I broke out, six-gun twirling,
to terrorize the ditches home.

Old habits still cramp me, awkward as ever
with slim pens, silverware and the fine touch of hands.
Even my sensitive friends take note.
They shadow this page with easy images
of rabbits, swans and flying birds.
Their wings flutter over the dark words.
*That ink will outlast the paper.*
Watch the handwriting float up and glide,
perfectly letter-spaced, nearly graceful,
the words you must imagine, to believe.

# Water Witch

## The Road to Erendira

Rough but passable he says,
waving a hairy California hand
at the road to Erendira.

His moustache gathers itself
from the cracks in his lips, and spit
fires at the red dirt.
The clay shrinks at your feet.

Choose a pair of ruts,
a file of thin cactus,
the road to Erendira.

The man you love smiles and waves
in return. Is it laughter that chokes?
Or only the dust
peppering the air between you.

You thought you leaned toward water,
always whispering your way in a wet accent.
The road to Erendira is deaf.

The car refuses another hill
oh the last to climb!
and the road becomes Erendira
and salt breeze easy on taut skin.

Stubborn creatures!
After seven years, can you place where you slept?
Each other's zip codes?

Remember. You stood
on the road to Erendira,
divided in half by the fiery sun
and your own tired shade.

## Young Man Returning

—after Denise Levertov's "A Young Man Travelling"

He returns, hair trimmed, beard
grown, to what he fears
is a place of disillusionment.
But now he shuns that
and all abstractions,
tries to sink them deep
as if into a swamp.
He feels the snow-melt mud
stick on his soles,
force his stride slow.
When his car slides away
from the skill in his hands, he curses
something other than this weather,
the road he thought familiar.
He is writing a story, he says,
not about heartbreak
but what could have been heartbreak.
As is his habit, he takes steps
two at a time,
but when he flings open the door
and grins at the woman
warming her hands at the stove
he catches his breath before he speaks,
blames the pounding in his ears
on drink, heavy meals
and the warm nights he meant to run
but stood on a square of sidewalk
staring it into Discovery Bay.

## A Stone's Throw

—after a painting by Arlene Lev

This fence marks the woman's border,
barbed wire, three strands,
ill-stretched and sagging. No reason
for a barrier, nothing
to hold in or back
but she lets it stay.
She leans on a fence post
and feels it shift
where it rots in the dirt.

The wind shifts.
At the entrance to his cabin
a patchwork quilt billows up the torn edge
where he ripped it through
as he would kick out a door.
When he told her that story
she watched herself in his eyes,
a tiny person bobbing on the dilated pupils.
They stood at the Y of the road,
divided by the untravelled brush
neither dares to call
No Man's Land.

They remember more
than they've ever shared.
She makes a fist to count again
the lines of marriage. So few
for a palm so marked.
She shrugs in answer to his raised eyebrows.
Their bodies move in rhythms prepared
to lessen the dissonance of speech.
Each word measures time,
finite and tragic.

Once they travelled to the city across the Sound.
She knew a gallery, pulled him
to look at a painting. *Read the title.*
                              *Isn't it wonderful?*

He mouths the words
against the air.
                    *Elective Affinity.*

Tonight they sleep in separate homes,
kindred images blinking against their eyelids.
They each select one to remember,
the blurred face of a wife, husband,
or the child lost
in the choked waking after dawn.

## Poverty Stricken at Ruby Beach

The ocean scums; sand hisses at our feet.
On this beach, the only thing whole
and clean is a sand dollar. I cannot
carry it; it is too cold,
and your hands fill my pockets.

*Antediluvian Love*

The grass poked her legs with damp spears.
Wet leaves smacked her face. She watched
his lovely body easing through the mist
and tried to forgive the rain with words.
"It doesn't matter," as the drops forced
through the ceiling, splattered like eggs
on the floor. "The garden will flourish,"
and the mud sucked her feet with fat lips.

One night the creek rose
and leveled the land silver
around their home. "How beautiful," she praised.
The silver moved. Animals
went along for the ride, raccoons bumped
the carcasses of calves, chickens whirled
like puffballs. "It can't be helped," she whispered
and carried Grandmother's tablecloth upstairs.

Now the house held an indoor swimming pool.
A river. An ocean. Fresh waves licked
at the stairs. She mumbled her last response
in this litany of Love and Water.
"We still have each other."
When she opened her eyes to accept his kiss,
she was alone in the attic.
Only for a moment she felt her mouth
cottonwood-dry with fear.

## Hoh Head

Dance between river and ocean,
feel the easy flow of water merge
with the hard salt pound of your heart.
Your footprints trail mud too far on the sand.
Yes, too far. The forest topples
into piles of driftwood. Bones twitch
to thrust outside the skin.
Drop to your knees and dig,
seek shelter, you hard-shelled creatures.

## The Process

After the exhilaration of choosing
and crushing the ripe berries, blend
and catalyze like an alchemist,
this is the next step—to strain
and siphon and watch the wine churn
to a new excitement.
The glass jugs line the table like pawns.
The game is incomplete.
I drop to my knees and study
the bubbles that foam the surface.
Turbulent as a new love—
this fermentation.

The wine will rest and clear.
The scent of yeast, familiar as a warm body,
leaves the house. Bottled and corked,
the wine ages
out of reach on a top shelf.
At times, a bottle rebels
and blows a cork, spattering wine
in the cupboard, on its neighbors.
Too much wild yeast in the air
and in me
bubbling my veins, stirring
my tongue. I could explode
in your arms. Where can I store myself
to settle and mellow?

In a few months, I will invite you
to my house to taste the blackberry wine,
dark and comfortable in the mouth
like the expectations
of an old friend.

*Outside City Limits*


Stung by nettles growing
under the stubborn alder log
in the first stage of rot,
she left the others
wielding noisy hatchets,
clearing the tangled, ancient path
to numb her hand in the creek.
She cradled her fingers
and watched the strenuous ax,
the red gallon of wine
meet the air with the flung limbs,
heard the stuttering hand saw
slice another branch,
the voices chant, "Our land! Our land!"
She leaped the creek,
traced the uncleared path
through mud and skunk cabbage
to a collapsed shed
and the honeysuckled frame of a Model T,
and at the ruined homestead
knelt, spread wide
her stinging fingers
and circled them around
one small, new tree.

## Through the Window of Apartment #3

Gray light
mutes the smudges on the glass,
softens the tiers of rooftops.
In the east, a cloud hooks,
a boomerang on return.
Watch it pale and straighten
as light pushes up
and streaks shadows on the frosted grass.

Learn from this: nothing in the air,
nothing flung, but my hands press against
and through the window, shards of glass
cupped in the palms, upturned, holding
what shattered, what will shatter,
prisms that catch and break
part of that sun into something beautiful,
if colors are beautiful
in thin strips, predictable
in arrangement. Even color-blind
I could name them. Sightless,
recite them.

Tell me that is better
than jagged glass
impaled in skin
receiving
what no one gives
what no one will take.

## Watching Out for Myself

As you will not see my body this year,
everywhere I move, I watch myself
for you, check my reflection
on parked cars and puddles.
I have lined my house with foil,
waxed and buffed the tile and polished
all utensils. My image bounces
off walls and floors. When I open
the cupboard, it leaps at me
like an ambush.

I sweat in a velvet caftan
with bits of glass
embroidered on it. When I sit,
the faces in my lap
mock me.
My sister would chide me
for my shiny nose. I scrub and scrape
until it gleams. Cross-eyed, I can just catch
a glimmer of my cheek on its flare.

Today, I sold the car, gave all my blood
to dip by body in platinum. Too late
I feel my eyelids glitter shut.
I am a mirror.
Waiting for your reflection
to creep across my bevelled edge,
I watch myself for you.

## The Sea Witch and the Mermaid

Nine purple oysters grip the tail
of the last mer-king's daughter.
The pain swims up
and through her body.
She feels the pinch on her fingertips,
the plucking at her eyelashes.
She remembers to swim proudly.

Transparent as ghosts, the fish maneuver
before her—so sheer she can see
their hearts beat against the glassy scales.
Bending its blades to that rhythm,
the seaweed twists a path for her.
No matter how fast her turn, how sharp
the angle, it marks her way.

Her blood is the last of a pale line—
no mer-princes for her to marry.
In the old story, she would visit
the sea witch, trade her liquid voice
for feet and choose the torment
of earth and men. There is no witch.
There is no choice.

On the ocean floor, the crabs are porcelain;
snails glow like the moon. Crusted
on a rock, gray foam camouflages
a clam. Once was a time
when mermaid bodies dissolved into foam
and burst to the surface, to spray
iridescent as a rainbow, intense as the sun.

## Striking Out

Believe the light, believe the eye,
the ant that detours a human foot.
She turns her face west, moves
as the sun would move
through slash and tight bushes
to the muddy clearing. Always a house,
unabandoned, a family of faces
knitted tight at the window.
Beyond, the watersick land falls down
to a brilliant sea.

Believe the curve of the earth,
those that swayed in ships and wagons
toward the end of water, the end of land.
The journey pulls not to an edge
or an inviting door
but here, on this open flat, where it began.
Still waving good-by,
the families group,
the backs of their hands clicking in time.
She tries to match the rhythm
but her hand thrusts out,
sure as a divining rod,
and the people part for her like the sea.

Believe wind, the air that kisses
then rips the skin.
A hawk dips behind the one man she remembers,
wings frame his head,
disappear at his throat.
Air sucks back

and the large sky swallows a talon,
a mask. Her wrist aches
from the weight she once carried
and a sudden gust pushes her to the ground.

Believe water in thin lines of rain,
the sheen on a leaf,
sweat.
At the river she lays nothing down
and drinks from one cupped hand.
The river is a crease in her palm.
She traces it upsteam,
chooses one small stream,
one source.

A choked sound escapes from the grasses
and waves shatter the shoreline.
In a tattered house, walls splinter
to etch out a map of the next country.
The road lights deep and straight
but she will clear her own path,
curving as the narrow stream curves.
On the river, people float down
on rented barges.
They are sleek and singing.
She believes their voices,
but lifts a fallen limb like another gate
and closes the path behind her.

*By Water Divined*


A pebble ripples the lake,
disturbs its determined smoothness.
Long after the small stone sinks
into the anonymous mud,
the lake shudders, convulsing upon itself.
Which is more beautiful?
The placid surface or the water that wavers,
transforming the image of a woman who leans
over the edge to watch the water stretch
then settle her features.

Still as the air she holds.
If a breeze whispers its way across the water,
it busies itself away from her,
leaving the fall of hair,
the drape of her clothing
in one smooth meld.
She remembers yearning for wind,
wind to scrape dry her cheeks
when the man with the fine guitar
plucked at her heart.

But as her tears dried
so did her heart.
The wind eroded her
like a poorly-tilled field
and she learned to wish for rain
and speak of crops, their yield separating
the good years from the bad.
She fears for the winter wheat, tempted
by unseasonable sun to appear too soon.
No human act can save it.

Still, she allows herself this indulgence,
makes the pilgrimage to the lake,

man-made, shallow,
but water enough to imagine
another geography, another kind of strife.
She splashes her face and waits
for wind and water to meet at her lips.
She has grafted herself to this land
where the cycle turns on harvest,
not death.

A last look at the water lifts her spirit,
reassures her that she shares
the ache of return with earth and weather.
Her breath quickens
and she sings, her voice a counterpoint
to the regularity of rise and fall,
the lone melodic line of plainsong,
a chant to celebrate the continuous ritual
that enters her words
that survives without her
that she sings.

*Biographical Note*

Kathleene West is the recipient of a 1983-84 Fulbright Fellowship at the University of Iceland. She has worked in the Poetry-in-the-Schools program in Nebraska and Washington and apprenticed as a letterpress printer with Copper Canyon Press and Abattoir Editions. She is currently enrolled in the doctoral program at the University of Nebraska/Lincoln. *Water Witching* is her fourth collection of poems.